MW01129337

Adaa's Story

The Remarkable Life of a Rescued Sea Otter

Rachel J.E. Sprague

Fathom Publishing

ISBN 978-1-954896-20-8 Hardcover
ISBN 978-1-954896-21-5 Paperback
ISBN 978-1-954896-22-2 e-book
Library of Congress Control Number 2023916408
Printed in United States of America

Photo credits
Alaska SeaLife Center: Connie Taylor
Seattle Aquarium: Rachel J.E. Sprague
Oregon Coast Aquarium: Oregon Coast Aquarium

Wildlife Permit
The Alaska SeaLife Center is permitted by the USFWS to rehabilitate and care for injured and abandoned sea otters. Adaa was rescued under the permit USFWS MA73419B-1.

Publisher's Cataloging-in-Publication data
Names: Sprague, Rachel J. E., author.
Title: Adaa's story : the remarkable life of a rescued sea otter / written and illustrated by Rachel J. E. Sprague.
Description: Anchorage, AK: Fathom Publishing Company, 2023. | Summary: Adaa begins life as an orphaned sea otter in Alaska. Through a chain of kindness, he is rescued and grows old at the Seattle Aquarium.
Identifiers: LCCN: 2023916408 | ISBN: 978-1-954896-20-8 (hardcover) | 978-1-954896-21-5 (paperback) | 978-1-954896-22-2 (ebook)
Subjects: LCSH Sea otter--Juvenile literature. | Marine life--Juvenile literature. | Wildlife rescue--Juvenile literature. | Wildlife rehabilitation--Juvenile literature. | Human-animal relationships--Juvenile literature. | BISAC JUVENILE NONFICTION / Animals / Animal Welfare | JUVENILE NONFICTION / Animals / Baby Animals | JUVENILE NONFICTION / Animals / Marine Life | JUVENILE NONFICTION / Animals / Zoos
Classification: LCC QL737.C25 .S78 2023 | DDC 599.74/447--dc23

RachelJESprague.com
Fathom Publishing
PO Box 200448
Anchorage, AK 99520
FathomPublishing.com

For Tyler, Violet and Eloise.

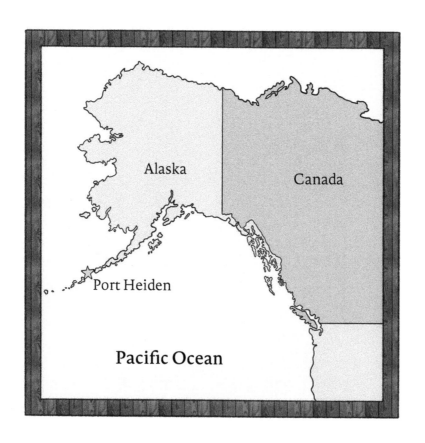

Alaska

Canada

Port Heiden

Pacific Ocean

Port Heiden, Alaska
January 2000

On a cold January morning in Alaska,
a baby sea otter is lost in the snow.

How did he get there? No one knows.
He is far from where an otter ought to be.

This sea otter needs care.
A call for help could save his life.

A rescue team arrives from Seward, Alaska.

They pull the baby sea otter from the snow.

They name him Adaa,* meaning "come ashore" in the Aleut language.

All are quiet as they watch. A story of kindness has begun.

* Pronounced AH-dah

Adaa now is in good care.
Kindness gives this otter wings.

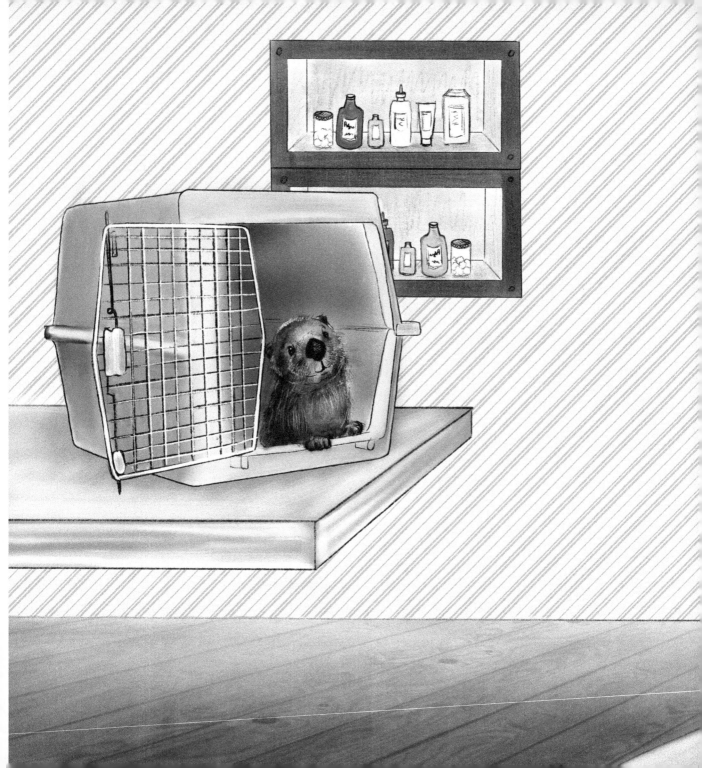

The rescue team takes Adaa to the Alaska SeaLife Center, a wildlife hospital where he can stay until he is healthy and strong.

He is not lonely here.

Through kindness comes healing.

And that healing can be joyful.

For several weeks, Adaa is cared for.
He needs to eat a lot.

He starts with a special formula
made for sea otter pups,
similar to milk …

… then graduates
to something more exciting.

Otters love to eat!

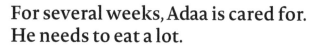

After mealtime, an otter ought to clean himself.
Adaa needs help with this at first.

Brushing, scrubbing, smoothing;
his coat begins to shine!

Bathing becomes his favorite pastime.

At the SeaLife Center, Adaa grows healthy and strong.

He is now ready for a new home.

Some animals are able to return to the wild after recovering. Adaa, however, was orphaned too young to know how to live in the wild.

Arrangements are made for him to move to an aquarium where he will be well cared for.

Traveling with a sea otter can be tricky!

They need lots of food,
and they need to stay clean.

It is also important that
a traveling otter doesn't get too hot.

A tub filled with ice
keeps Adaa cool and
comfortable on his
long journey to the
aquarium.

Adaa travels first to the Oregon Coast Aquarium.

Then he moves again.
The Seattle Aquarium becomes his forever home.

At the aquarium, Adaa is surrounded
by all sorts of interesting creatures.

But best of all …

... he now has a family.

Adaa may feel nervous at first,
but his new family will help him feel safe.

Through kindness
comes trust.

Together they eat.

Together they brush and scrub and smooth their coats
until they shine.

They live together for years doing all the
things that sea otters ought to do,
cared for by the aquarium staff.

Those years are filled with joy.

The most amazing thing happens:

This sea otter who started life alone
and lost in the snow,
gets the chance to grow old.

Very, very old.

As an old otter, Adaa spends his afternoons sleeping under a cool blanket of Seattle rain.

In his dreams, he remembers
the story of his life;
where he began and
who helped him along the way.

But how will his story end?

One day a rescue team arrives.

They have pulled a baby sea otter from a fishing net.
Her name is Mishka, meaning "little bear."

Mishka has so much to learn.
Mishka will need so much care.

Adaa has found the ending to his story.
All are quiet as they watch.

Another story of kindness begins.

Adaa 1999-2022

Adaa's Story is based on the life of the Seattle Aquarium's most famous sea otter. The real Adaa was found in January 2000 on a runway in Port Heiden, Alaska, when he was about four months old. Having been separated from his mother at such an early age, his chance of survival in the wild was very low.

Lucky for Adaa, the Alaska SeaLife Center in Seward was notified and a wildlife response team came quickly to his rescue.

After recovering at the Alaska SeaLife Center, Adaa's first move out of Alaska was to the Oregon Coast Aquarium where he received further care and training. In 2004, he moved to the Seattle Aquarium which became his permanent home.

While Adaa was never able to return to the wild due to his rocky start in life, his years at the aquarium allowed him to have a family of his own and become an ambassador of sea otter conservation, loved by all.

In his later years, Adaa only grew more and more beloved by the aquarium community as they watched him bond with a younger sea otter, Mishka, who had also been orphaned and was found in a fishing net.

At the time of his death, Adaa was just over twenty-two years old; the oldest male sea otter on record with the Association of Zoos and Aquariums. Adaa's long and healthy life is a tribute to the people and organizations who cared for him.

Adaa's Journey

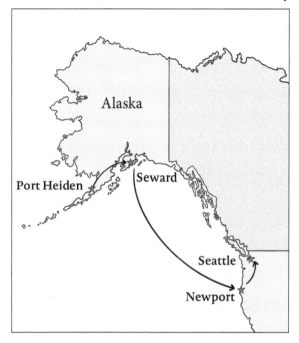

The Alaska SeaLife Center is a non-profit organization that combines a public aquarium with marine research, education, and wildlife response. It is the only permanent marine mammal rescue and rehabilitation facility in Alaska. Learn more at alaskasealife.org. The Alaska SeaLife Center is permitted by the USFWS to rehabilitate and care for injured and abandoned sea otters. Adaa was rescued under the permit USFWS MA73419B-1.

The Seattle Aquarium is a non-profit organization with the mission: Inspiring Conservation of the Marine Environment. It strives to increase awe and understanding of the ocean. Learn more about what you can do to help sea otters at SeattleAquarium.org.

The Oregon Coast Aquarium is a nonprofit organization with the mission to create engaging experiences that connect visitors to the Oregon coast and inspire ocean conservation.

What to do if you Find a Stranded Sea Otter?

◆ Do NOT try to touch it or catch it.

◆ Keep people and pets at least 50 yards away from it.

◆ Immediately contact your local wildlife response organization.

◆ Visit the NOAA Fisheries website for a list of who to call in your area. www.fisheries.noaa.gov/report

Fun Facts about Sea Otters

Life Span   Most northern sea otters in the wild live to be around 15-20 years old. Adaa lived to be over 22 years old, the oldest male sea otter on record!

Size   Sea otters are the smallest marine mammal in North America. They weigh 45 to 90 pounds.

Diet   Their diet includes clams, crabs, mussels, fish, and sea urchins. They use rocks as "tools" to crack open their food, and they can eat while floating on their backs in the water. They eat 25 percent of their body weight every day!

Grooming   Sea otters have the thickest fur of any animal on earth. They have up to one million hairs per square inch. Most marine mammals have a layer of blubber for warmth. Sea otters do not. They rely on their thick fur to keep warm. They spend a lot of time every day grooming which helps trap air and heat.

<u>Juvenile Sea Otters</u> Otter pups stay with the mother for about six months, carried on the mother's belly in the water. They have such dense baby fur that they can't dive underwater. Often the mothers will leave the pups safely floating, wrapped in a strand of kelp so they don't float away, while the mothers dive for food. A group of sea otters floating together is called a raft.

<u>Protections</u> Sea otters were nearly hunted to extinction by fur traders in the 19th century. Today they are protected by the Marine Mammal Protection Act and the Endangered Species Act.

<u>Keystone Species</u> Sea otters are considered a "keystone species." This means that sea otters play a very important role in keeping their home ecosystems healthy and balanced. Without sea otters, the kelp forests that provide shelter to so many sea creatures would be destroyed by sea urchins.

Watch Sea Otters Online

Monterey Bay Aquarium
montereybayaquarium.org/animals/live-cams/sea-otter-cam

Oregon Coast Aquarium
aquarium.org/live-cameras/otter-cam

Seattle Aquarium
seattleaquarium.org/live-cams

Vancouver Aquarium
vanaqua.org/explore/animals/sea-otters/#seaottercam

Where do Sea Otters Live?

It is believed that about ninety percent of the world's sea otters live in Alaska's coastal waters. Sea otters are also found in shallow waters of the Northern Pacific Ocean down through California and along the coastlines of Russia.

What does the Future Look Like for Sea Otters?

Sea otters are slowly making a comeback in the wild, although some populations are still threatened. Aquariums around the country such as the Seattle Aquarium continue to home orphaned otters and educate the public about the importance of saving these creatures.

The Monterey Bay Aquarium is the first of its kind to successfully place baby sea otters with surrogate mothers. These female otters teach the pups the skills they need to eventually survive on their own in the wild.

Visit Sea Otters at the Aquarium

Alaska SeaLife Center
alaskasealife.org
Seward, Alaska

Aquarium of the Pacific
aquariumofpacific.org
Long Beach, California

The Marine Mammal Center
marinemammalcenter.org
Sausalito, California

Monterey Bay Aquarium
montereybayaquarium.org
Monterey, California

Oregon Coast Aquarium
aquarium.org
Newport, Oregon

Pittsburgh Zoo & Aquarium
pittsburghzoo.org
Pittsburgh, Pennsylvania

Seattle Aquarium
seattleaquarium.org
Seattle, Washington

Shedd Aquarium
sheddaquarium.org
Chicago, Illinois

Vancouver Aquarium
vanaqua.org
Vancouver, British Columbia

About the Author

Rachel J.E. Sprague writes and illustrates out of her home in Seattle, Washington. As a trained natural science illustrator, she gains inspiration from the plants and animals around her. She loves collaborating with scientists and is passionate about bringing the arts and sciences together through her work. In her free time, she likes to explore the forests and beaches of the Pacific Northwest with her family.

www.racheljesprague.com
instagram.com/racheljesprague
Teacher's Guide and Children's Activities at www.fathompublishing.com

Printed in the USA
CPSIA information can be obtained
at www.ICGtesting.com
LVHW062149161123
764155LV00012B/167

9 781954 896208